Original title:
Rhymes of the Rainforest

Copyright © 2025 Creative Arts Management OÜ
All rights reserved.

Author: Nash Everly
ISBN HARDBACK: 978-1-80567-248-7
ISBN PAPERBACK: 978-1-80567-547-1

Nocturnal Notes in the Green

Under the moon, the frogs croak loud,
Crickets perform for a curious crowd.
The owls can't quite keep up with the beat,
While fireflies dance on little light feet.

A raccoon sneaks snacks with quite a flair,
In the middle of midnight, there's music to share.
Lizards break-dance on mossy old logs,
As bats play tag with the giddy frogs.

Chants of the Colorful Canopy

Parrots squawk fashion tips from above,
While toucans strike poses, it's true love.
Monkeys swing in with quite a show,
Teaching the trees to do the limbo flow.

Each leaf whispers secrets, and giggles ensue,
While chameleons boast in a dazzling hue.
The kapok tree wiggles its branches and sway,
As the sloths move in slow-mo, inviting the play.

Spotlight on the Silent Sentries

The jaguar naps with a blush of pride,
Yet dreams of racing, though nowhere to hide.
While stoic turtles with shells so bright,
Join in the chorus of day turning night.

Leaping lizards join in the dance of the fun,
While ants march along, forming lines on the run.
With a squeaky old parrot relaying the news,
Each creature can't stop prancing in shoes.

Nature's Whirlwind of Sound

A symphony plays in the leaves above,
With drumming by beetles, it's pure love.
Breezes whistle tunes while vines twist and curl,
As dancing insects give laughter a whirl.

Rain taps a beat that's never too shy,
While the breeze hums softly with a sigh.
Each sound is a riddle, a giggle, a game,
In this jungle where everyone knows your name.

Prayers of the Prowling Creatures

In shadows deep where whispers creep,
A jaguar frets, loses sleep.
He prays for mice with cheese to find,
And dreams of snacks, both large and kind.

The monkeys laugh and shake the trees,
While parrots squawk with such great ease.
They gather round, a motley crew,
To swap their tales of nighttime stew.

The Heartbeat of Humid Nights

The frogs perform a symphony,
With croaks that sound like harmony.
They leap and croon with sheer delight,
While bugs pass by, avoiding fright.

Fireflies dance like tiny stars,
Engaging in their nightly spar.
Each flicker's glow, a silly jig,
A twirl for all, both small and big.

Fables from the Forest Floor

A turtle with a shiny shell,
Claims he can swim quite well, oh swell!
But when he dove, he lost his hat,
And left the fish all laughing flat.

An ant in boots, so rare and neat,
Parades around on tiny feet.
With every step, a grand parade,
He stomps and squeaks, a funny charade.

The Heart of the Jungle's Song

A sloth hung high, in branches swayed,
In dreams of speed, he often played.
He thinks he's fast, though all around,
His love for naps is fiercely bound.

The toucan sports a vibrant beak,
With fruit for lunch, he thinks he's sleek.
He tries to flirt with every vine,
But just ends up in a banana line.

Trinkets of the Treetops' Treasure

A squirrel found a shiny thing,
He thought it must be fit for kings.
He wore it like a little crown,
Until it rolled, and he fell down.

A toucan laughed and said, "Oh dear!"
"Your royal days just disappeared!"
They chuckled 'neath the leafy light,
As branches swayed, a funny sight.

Amidst the vines, a monkey swings,
Collecting all the jingly blings.
He tied them to his fruit-filled hat,
And danced around, how about that?

Together they created tunes,
With trinkets gleaned from afternoon.
The jungle echoed with their cheer,
As laughter rang from far and near.

Whispers of Wisdom in the Wilderness

An old frog croaks a sage's lore,
Beneath the branches, close to the floor.
"Avoid the snakes that like to tease,
And never chat among the trees."

A parrot squawked, "But what is wise?"
"To not eat fruit that's full of flies!"
They pondered deep with twinkling eyes,
As mischief danced in their replies.

A sloth chimed in, somewhat bemused,
"I take my time, and that's my muse.
Life's too fast, so let it flow,
Just hang around, and take it slow!"

The others giggled, thoughts awash,
"Old frog's wisdom, a total posh!"
With every word, they learned a lot,
Not every tale needs to be hot.

Pattering Petals and Pensive Ferns

The petals danced in rain's bright song,
While ferns just sighed, "We feel so strong!"
A caterpillar joined the game,
Declaring, "I'll win the best name!"

The petals laughed, "Oh, what is that?"
While ferns just swayed, their thoughts fell flat.
The caterpillar smiled and said,
"I'll soon be beautiful instead!"

With every squiggle, every move,
The petals cheered, their joy to prove.
All nature joined this merry spree,
As laughter thrived, wild and free!

In puddles formed, the petals twirled,
The ferns just sighed, "We are unfurled."
They swayed along with dreamer's tunes,
Creating smiles in afternoon's boon.

Echoes of Enchantment and Earth

A chorus of frogs sang on a log,
While beating drums like a jungle hog.
They croaked and ribbited with flair,
Each note a splash, like they just don't care!

The beetles clapped their tiny hands,
Creating music no one understands.
A snake slithered, joined the show,
With every groove, he'd steal the glow!

The howler monkeys shouted loud,
"We're best performers in this crowd!"
With chants and cheers, they stole the scene,
While flowers bloomed in colors keen.

At dusk, the magic seemed to grow,
With echoes dancing to and fro.
Both night and nature sighed with glee,
As rhythms rolled through every tree.

A Canvas of Colorful Creatures

In the jungle, critters dance,
With polka dots and stripes by chance.
A parrot's hat, a monkey's shoes,
Who knew fashion thrived in hues?

Frogs wear crowns, snapping selfies,
Lizards gossip, feeling wealthy.
A toucan juggles fruit with glee,
"Move aside!" says the bumblebee!

Amid the leaves, they throw a ball,
While sloths just chill, they're late to call.
The jungle parties, wild and free,
With laughter ringing from each tree!

A canvas spied through leafy lanes,
Where joy is found in clever gains.
As every creature finds its role,
They paint with flair, they steal the show!

The Map of Memories in Moss

On soft green ground where secrets lie,
The mossy map will make you sigh.
A pebble's tale, a twig's delight,
Where lost explorers find their sight.

"Oh look!" yells one, "an acorn here!"
The squirrels cheer, they hold it dear.
Tiny roads made from snails' trails,
As nature sends its funny tales.

A squirrel flips through its memory book,
While toads rehearse with crazy looks.
The map of laughs in every clump,
Beneath the ferns, life's little bump.

Old turtles softly reminisce,
"Remember when? Oh, that was bliss!"
With every squishy squelch, they grin,
Their stories whisper, let the fun begin!

Flavors of Flora and Fables

Candy flowers bloom with flair,
Chocolate vines float in the air.
Gummy bears dance with delight,
As licorice snakes slither at night.

Tasty tales of fruit with zest,
Bananas challenge, "I'm the best!"
Berries giggle, in a stew,
While cupcakes chat, "We're the crew!"

Peaches share a juicy tale,
As popcorn trees sway without fail.
A jolly feast on sunny days,
Where pastries prance in silly ways.

Sweet aromas fill the breeze,
With laughter buzzing through the trees.
In this land of flavors spry,
It's a feast, no need to fly!

The Lietmotif of Life's Canvas

In the woods, the rhythm hums,
With nature's beat, the fun becomes.
The tap of feet, the clap of wings,
It's time for all to dance and sing!

The wind sweeps through, a playful tease,
As shadows sway with utmost ease.
A family of ants on parade,
Their tiny moves never fade.

A jaguar joins with a swaggering strut,
While iguanas say, "What's up?"
Each heartbeat jives, and hearts align,
In this canvas, feel divine!

Laughter echoes, the mixing sound,
As cheers rise high from every ground.
In each corner, life's a thrill,
Where colors dance and hearts fulfill!

Enchanted Echoes in the Underbrush

A monkey swung with style and grace,
He tripped on vines, oh what a face!
The parrot laughed, it was quite the scene,
A dance-off happened, you know what I mean!

The frogs started croaking a wacky tune,
While bats grooved under the bright full moon.
An iguana sighed, 'This disco's my jam!'
Everyone joined in, 'Let's groove, yes we can!'

Ballad of the Blooming Flowers

The daisies argued who's the best,
While tulips laughed and took a rest.
A sunflower turned and made a face,
'You think you're cute? Let's pick up the pace!'

The bees buzzed in, all dressed in bling,
'We're the judges of this flowering fling!'
Petals swayed, in a colorful brawl,
Who knew gardens could hold such a ball?

Stories from the Shaded Pathways

A sly little fox sat down for a chat,
With a wise old turtle who wore a hat.
They shared wild tales of dance and despair,
While squirrels flipped acorns through the air.

Suddenly a deer joined with a hop,
'Let's throw a party, right on the top!'
The shadows giggled and joined in the feat,
Together they danced to an offbeat beat.

The Choral Call of Cascading Water

The waterfall sang in a splishy-splash,
While frogs joined in with a ribbity flash.
Fish twirled around, all in a line,
'Isn't this music simply divine?'

But then came a splash from a clumsy bear,
Who thought he could join, but fell in fair!
With a bubbly grunt, he came to the shore,
'Next time I'll dance, I promise, I swore!'

The Pulse of Petals in the Rain

In a jungle lush and bright,
Petals dance with pure delight,
Droplets bounce on leafy crowns,
While frogs wear tiny, silly frowns.

Swaying vines in a funky beat,
A parrot struts on vibrant feet,
The monkeys giggle, swinging high,
While snails are zooming, oh my, oh my!

When the rain begins to play,
All the critters join the fray,
Slugs in capes that glisten wide,
Jiving with the river's tide.

At twilight, all the fun's not done,
With fireflies flickering, oh what fun!
In this green world, we can't complain,
Joining in the pulse of rain.

Canopy Murmurs and Moonlit Dreams

Moonlit beams on leafy beds,
Whispers dance right above our heads,
Squirrels giggle at midnight snacks,
While raccoons plot their daring hacks.

The owls, wise, wear funny shades,
Arguing 'bout their favorite glades,
With every hoot, a joke they crack,
As shadows flicker, no one looks back.

From up above, the stars align,
Critters pause to drink their wine,
A toucan tells the best old tales,
Of fish in hats and four-legged snails.

In dreams, we glide on magic wings,
Beneath the moon and silly things,
Through leafy paths and laughter's streams,
Finding joy in starlit dreams.

Stories Beneath the Starlit Boughs

Underneath the towering trees,
Listen close to giggles in the breeze,
Fireflies tell their tales of yore,
As crickets stomp and demand encore.

With wise old owls as the crowd,
Each story told with laughter loud,
A chameleon pretends to cry,
Forgetting where he hid, oh my!

Beneath the stars, the fables grow,
Of dancing sloths and friendly glow,
Swinging branches, a show of sight,
Making visions that feel just right.

So gather 'round, let stories flow,
In these woods, the fun's a show,
Each leafy bough, a stage so grand,
With cosmic laughs across the land.

Secrets of the Silken Spider's Web

In the morning, dew drops shine,
A spider's silk, a perfect line,
Where all her friends come by and chat,
Discussing pizza, fish, and that!

A beetle struts, all dressed in flair,
Says, "You'd love my new doughnut hair!"
While ants march by in perfect rows,
Arguing which way the river flows.

With each twist, the web does sway,
Where silly critters come to play,
A banana peel as dance floor cool,
Get ready for the funniest duel.

The secrets shared are light as air,
From sticky traps to silly hair,
In this web of jolly cheer,
Laughter echoes far and near.

Chants from the Chattering Tree Frogs

A frog on a branch, quite the comedian,
Ribbits and croaks, a full-blown median.
He tells all the flies, 'You can't outrun me!'
While tripping on leaves like a sprightly glee.

Jumps in a puddle, making a splash,
Googly-eyed critters dash in a flash.
'Catch me if you can!' the jovial chap sings,
As beetles just giggle, on tiny wings.

Frogs in a choir, what a funny sight,
Croaking their tunes through the darkened night.
With mischief and laughter we join their spree,
In this leafy theatre, wild and free.

Swinging with joy, they're quite the delight,
A slippery stage, their antics ignite.
So listen closely, let the fun unfold,
With each little croak, more laughter is told.

Tides of Tranquility in the Tropics

A parrot named Pete, with feathers so bright,
Steals bananas and giggles, what a silly sight!
He squawks to the monkeys, 'Come share my treat!'
While juggling some mangoes, he can't find his seat.

The sloths moving slow, with a chuckle and grin,
Race on a twig, though they won't ever win.
'Join our slow dance!' it's an all-day affair,
As their buddy the toucan just takes to the air.

The sun sets low, the jokes start to grow,
Crickets provide laughs, in a rhythmic show.
They chirp 'til they're hoarse, each note filled with fun,
While shadows creak softly, 'Where's everyone?'

At the edge of the lagoon, a puddle's surprise,
Our friends do a splash, reaching for the skies.
In a whirl of giggles, they end the day,
In this tropical haven, where laughter will stay.

Whirling with the Wind in the Wild

A squirrel named Sam, with a nut in his mouth,
Flips through the branches, heading south.
He somersaults wide, then tumbles on down,
While laughing at shadows, he owns the whole town.

The breeze starts to dance, through leaves it will sway,
Delighting the critters who decide to play.
An owl in a hat shouts, 'Time for a ball!'
As fireflies gather, one and all.

The winds whisper secrets to bushes and trees,
Letting the giggles float softly with ease.
Bunnies hop high, doing flips in the air,
Join the woodland waltz—no worry, no care.

A tornado of fun, we spin and we twirl,
As nature's own music begins to unfurl.
With laughter cascading, like rain from the sky,
In this wild revelry, spirits soar high.

Symphony of Sprites and Shadows

The sprites flit and flutter, with wings all aglow,
Creating a ruckus, while putting on a show.
With cider and giggles, they share their bright cheer,
As shadows chime in, whispering, 'We're here!'

A gnome with a grin starts to tickle the night,
Beneath the tall ferns, oh what a sight!
The nocturnal dance, they sway with delight,
Glowing like lanterns, they shine in twilight.

A frog and a sprite share a laugh on a leaf,
With a belly full of giggles, they've conquered their grief.
While shadows clap hands, in rhythm and rhyme,
In their silly parade, they're dancing through time.

As the moon keeps on winking, they twirl one last spin,
A symphony echoing, laughter bursts within.
So hush now dear friend, the night bids goodbye,
In this woodsy wonderland, under the sky.

Secrets Written on the Water's Edge

Whispers echo where frogs croak,
Turtles slide, and tree limbs poke.
Fish giggle in their silvery dance,
While crickets plan their next romance.

A monkey slips, oh what a sight,
Splashing down, a comical fright.
The otter laughs, shows off its flair,
As the snail claims it's still not there.

Duet of Dawn and Dusk in the Wild

Morning yawns with bright, pink skies,
While sleepy bats rub sleepy eyes.
The parrot squawks a silly tune,
And the sun beams down like a cartoon.

As dusk arrives, the fireflies flash,
Bidding farewell to the day with a splash.
Frogs leap high in a bouncing spree,
Underneath the giggling banyan tree.

Chasing the Shadows of Serenity

A sloth moves with great delight,
But I think it's napping out of sight.
The jaguar winks, takes a chance,
And the capybara just wants to dance.

Underneath leaves that dance and sway,
Lizards wear sunglasses, brightening the day.
A chatty parrot spills all the tea,
About what the toucan saw by the tree.

Lull of the Leaves in the Lush

The wind whispers secrets to the trees,
Making them giggle like playful bees.
A squirrel juggles acorns with glee,
While the rabbit sips tea under a spree.

The foliage rustles, a playful sigh,
As the butterfly asks, "Why so shy?"
With blooms winking under the sun,
Every critter's ready for a bit of fun.

Whirlpools of Whispers in the Green

In the jungle, a frog sings,
Bouncing high on elastic springs.
Birds giggle at his silly dance,
Wondering if he'll find romance.

Trees gossip about passing ants,
Who wear tiny, mismatched pants.
Monkeys tease with cheeky grins,
Hiding nuts where the fun begins.

Lizards laugh on sunlit rocks,
As the turtle forgets his socks.
Bouncing berries roll down the hill,
Who knew fruit could bring such a thrill?

So if you wander through the trees,
Prepare to laugh and catch the breeze.
Nature's folly is here to share,
With all the critters unaware.

Enchanted Verses of the Hidden Hollow

In a hollow, a hedgehog sings,
With spines that dance like wobbly springs.
Squirrels giggle at his tune,
Sipping nectar from a flower's balloon.

A parrot tries to crack a joke,
But only the vines seem to poke.
Each leaf chuckles with delight,
At the sight of the clumsy kite.

Crickets chirp in rhythmic beats,
While ants boogie on wobbly feet.
A butterfly just can't pick a side,
As it twirls in a colorful glide.

All the critters begin to cheer,
For the laughter they hold so dear.
In this hollow, the day feels bright,
With giggles echoing into the night.

Footsteps of the Forest's Memory

Footsteps echo in the glade,
Where a gopher wears a sun hat made.
He shuffles through the leaves so sly,
Making acorns cook as pies.

A snail boasts of its speedy race,
Claiming it's the champion of the place.
But the cockroach buzzes back with flair,
Saying, 'I'll beat you, if I dare!'

The raccoon plays a clever game,
Searching for treasures, oh what a shame!
When he finds himself in a bean,
Taking off like a sticky teen.

With every story, a giggle's sparked,
As tails and tales of life are marked.
In this memory of leafy dreams,
The laughter flows like playful streams.

Tales Intertwined in the Understory

In the understory, a tale spins round,
A sloth with dreams of wearing a crown.
He practices his royal wave,
But all the branches start to cave!

A toucan cheers with its bright beak,
As the sloth grumbles in a sleepy squeak.
Each word is an adventure told,
In a forest where laughter unfolds.

Chattering frogs join the parade,
With their croaks making quite a charade.
They leap and hop with a flair so grand,
Making sure to spread joy across the land.

So come and dance under the trees,
Join in the mirth and playful tease.
In this undergrowth of giggles galore,
We'll share our stories forevermore!

Echoing Through the Emerald Labyrinth

In the jungle, monkeys swing,
They tease the birds that like to sing.
A parrot splats with a funny squawk,
While sloths just hang and take a walk.

The trees all giggle when it's wet,
As frogs jump high without a fret.
A jaguar sneezes, oh what a scene,
While chattering squirrels plot like a team.

From leaf to leaf, the chimes they go,
As ants march on in a perfect row.
The humidity raises a silly cheer,
With laughter ringing loud and clear.

In this maze of green delight,
Even the insects dance at night.
With every rustle, the humor spreads,
A giggling forest, where joy embeds.

Soliloquy of Sunlight and Serenity

Sunbeams filter through the leaves,
Creating shadows, where humor weaves.
A lighthearted breeze playfully shakes,
While a toucan stares, and then it quakes.

The breeze whispers jokes to everything near,
As chattering critters perk up to hear.
An iguana bursts with a comedic pout,
Declaring, "I'm fabulous! No doubt!"

In the canopy high, there's tales to tell,
Of dancing vines and a turtle's shell.
Where sunlight shines, it's quite a sight,
As the frogs put on shows with all their might.

With every shimmer, the laughter grows,
In a paradise where silliness flows.
And while the world spins and sways, it seems,
Nature chuckles in glorious dreams.

The Call of the Canopied Horizon

Underneath the sprawling trees,
A rascal raccoon snatches a breeze.
He thinks he's sly, but oh my dear,
The monkeys laugh, they're always near.

With leaves like hats, the bugs parade,
Unaware they're part of the great charade.
An excited thump brings a moment of fright,
As the frogs burst out in a frog-leap fight!

The colors pop like a painter's box,
With splashes of laughter emerging from the rocks.
A turtle trips and lands on a vine,
Waving, he quips, "Oh, I'm just fine!"

In the horizon's call, they sway and jive,
With every mishap, they feel alive.
The spirits of joy, forever entwined,
In this canopy where laughter's designed.

Vignettes of the Vibrant Wilderness

In the wild, where the critters chatter,
Each moment's a giggle, each mishap a matter.
A parrot yells jokes that are quite absurd,
While the toucan joins in—how absurdly heard!

The fireflies twinkle, like stars in a dance,
While a lizard stumbles in a silly prance.
A frog on a leaf is telling a tale,
Of slippery ways to avoid the snail.

The chorus of giggles breaks all the quiet,
Even the turtles partake in the riot.
Where every creature has something to share,
In this colorful world, with humor to spare.

The wilderness whispers with every sound,
Filling the air with joy all around.
In playful antics, the wilderness plays,
Where life's a jest, in delightful displays.

Wind's Embrace in the Dense Divide

The wind whispers secrets, oh so sly,
Leaves giggle softly, as they flutter by.
A squirrel in a hat, taking a grand leap,
Tripping on his tail, into bushes he'll creep.

The vines dance cha-cha, in a leafy parade,
While frogs hold a contest in the cool shade.
With each little croak, they all start to cheer,
Who knew that croaking could bring such good cheer?

Filters of Light Through Layers of Life

Sunbeams peek through, like a kid's sunny grin,
Tickling the shadows where the critters all spin.
A ladybug disco, with spots all aglow,
Jive to the rhythm of the flowing flow.

The chatter of monkeys, in trees they convene,
Playing expert tag, like a wild circus scene.
Each branch holds a promise for laughter to grow,
Swinging in joy, just putting on a show.

The Dreaming Drum of Distant Birds

Birds drum on the branches, a wild, funny tune,
Each beat is a giggle, with a splash of moon.
A parrot in goggles, adding flair to the band,
Sings out a solo, oh isn't it grand?

With feathers so bright, they lead a parade,
A funky formation, in the light and the shade.
Each fluttering friend, has a tale to weave,
In this riotous concert, you wouldn't believe!

Ballads at the Base of the Banyan

At the sturdy root, where the shadows all play,
The critters are crooning, right there every day.
A turtle in sunglasses strumming a tune,
While the ants tap dance, oh what a festoon!

A squirrel brings snacks, making all the friends cheer,
Gathering around, drawing everyone near.
With laughter resounding and stories to tell,
Underneath the banyan, all's merry and well.

Serenade of the Soaked Foliage

In a leafy green jungle, oh what a sight,
The frogs all croak loudly, their voices in flight.
A parrot's bright colors, a chatty delight,
While monkeys do somersaults, oh what a height!

But watch out for raindrops, they plop and they splat,
As sloths drop their snacks, and they squish with a splat.
The plants are all laughing, they tip their green hats,
Saying, 'We love a good party, just look at that cat!'

Murmurs in the Misty Understory

A slippery snail slides, with a grin and a glide,
While toucans are gossiping, feathers bonafide.
'Who wore it best?' they caw, full of pride,
In this vibrant green realm, where secrets abide.

A cheeky old jaguar yawns, not much to do,
'Why run with the herd, when you can snooze too?'
With a flip of his tail, he claims a fine view,
While frogs start a conga, made just for the zoo!

Tapestry of the Tropical Thicket

Lizards play tag on the branches up high,
While a slapping old toucan gives winged high-fives.
Rainbow-hued geckos make costumes, oh my!
The fun never ends where the monkeys arrive.

Rats dance with delight in their polka-dot shoes,
As orchids burst forth in their colorful hues.
With laughter that echoes, they sing out the blues,
In a wacky world where there's nothing to lose!

Hymn of the Highwood

The wind tickles palms, they giggle and sway,
While squirrels tell tales of their acorn buffet.
Under twinkling stars, they boogie and play,
As the moon gives a wink, 'Just be silly today!'

A chorus of crickets joins in on the fun,
With fireflies dancing, they glow, one by one.
So come take a stroll, where the laughter's begun,
In this tropical circus, we all are the sun!

Voices of the Verdant Depths

In the jungle, a frog sings a tune,
With a croak and a leap beneath the moon.
A parrot mimics with all of its might,
Saying "Hello!" to a very surprised kite.

The sloth moves slow with a cheeky grin,
Hanging from branches, it's ready to win.
A toucan drops fruit in a prankster's style,
And the whole canopy bursts into smiles!

The chattering monkeys throw jokes all around,
While the jaguar grins, barely making a sound.
Even the trees in their rooted stance,
Join in laughter, as branches sway and dance.

So here in the depths, where the creatures play,
Every moment's a giggle in the green ballet.
With fun in the air and whimsy in sight,
The jungle's a stage, full of pure delight!

Lullabies of the Lush

The crickets chirp a soothing beat,
While the bush babies bounce to a sleepy seat.
A lazy sloth sings softly off key,
In the middle of night, with a cup of sweet tea.

A parakeet tries to hum a nice song,
But it fluffs its feathers and gets all wrong.
The frogs join in with a ribbit parade,
Creating a chorus, perfectly made!

With a swish and a splash, the river agrees,
Whispering secrets through the rustling leaves.
As the moon dips low, and the stars start to wink,
All the animals settle—don't you think?

So close your eyes to the lullaby's flow,
As the jungle hums soft, in the nighttime glow.
The world may be funny, with giggles and glee,
But in this night song, we dream wild and free!

Nature's Hidden Harmonies

A buzzing bee in a flowered hat,
Sings an offbeat tune, just imagine that!
While the ants march past in a single file,
Telling jokes to each other with an organized smile.

The chameleon's colors change with each pun,
While the monkeys swing by, truly having fun.
A jaguar chuckles, almost in jest,
As a tapir slips, facing nature's test.

The river giggles at stones it meets,
With splashes that dance to rhythmic beats.
Even the wind seems to silently laugh,
Twisting through trees like a whimsical draft.

In this symphony of wild, oh so bright,
Where jokes are exchanged with sheer delight,
The creatures all gather and sway in a trance,
Singing together, in this goofy dance!

Tales from the Twisted Roots

In twisted roots, where mischief unfolds,
A wise old turtle with humor retolds.
He sat on a log with a grin so wide,
Sharing stories of the fawns, trying to hide.

A snake slithered by, with a bad joke or two,
"Why don't we ever play cards, who knew?"
The frogs just ribbited, rolling their eyes,
While the sloth watched on—oh, the nature of lies!

The jaguar pranks the parrot aflight,
Telling tall tales that caused quite a fright.
And the colorful beetle, proud of his hues,
Joined in the laughter with some quirky news.

So under the canopy, stories are spun,
Filled with chuckles, led by the sun.
In these twisted roots, where wisdom is found,
Funny little tales keep our laughter unbound!

The Language of Leaves in Lush Lore

In whispers soft, the leaves like to chat,
They gossip about the size of the cat.
The vines twist and twirl in a flowery jest,
Saying, "I'm the best, but the fronds do protest!"

Beneath the bright sun, the cacti turn red,
Complaining about thorns in a snarky thread.
The flowers all laugh at the sloth's funny stare,
As he drags his feet like he hasn't a care!

A parrot squawks tales of a squirrel's mistake,
Claiming he hopped on a buttercup cake.
Yet a monkey swings by with a cheeky parade,
Saying, "I'll swing straight, watch the fun I've made!"

So each leaf grins, in the warm, sunny glade,
In the jungle of jokes, there's never a shade.
The sounds of their laughter float bright through the trees,

And echo around with the buzz of the bees!

Breath of the Riverine Spirits

The river hums softly, a splishy splash tune,
It dances with ripples beneath the bright moon.
Frogs croak in harmony, a wacky delight,
As fish throw a party, sunbathing at night!

A turtle swims by with a grin on his face,
He's running a race, at an unhurried pace.
"Who's slow and steady?" the otter then plays,
"With a wiggle and wiggle, let's brighten their days!"

The willows all sway, wearing crowns made of mist,
While crickets hold concerts that very few missed.
They chirp little ditties that brighten the gloom,
As the stars above gather like flowers in bloom!

So if you should wander where the waters reflect,
You'll find spirits laughing and joy to collect.
From rock to the willow, let the good times flow,
Where humor and rivers put on quite a show!

Fables of Ferns and Feathers

The ferns flap their fronds and begin to declare,
"Who needs to be tall when you're springy and fair?"
A toucan, so proud with a colorful beak,
Says, "I'm writing a book; it's the highlight of the week!"

The owls hoot aloud, wearing glasses for style,
As they ponder deep thoughts, but can't help but smile.
They snicker at rabbits who jump without grace,
Telling tall tales of a frog in a race!

Each feathered friend fluffs, and they burst out in song,
Celebrating all the rights of the wrong.
With chatter so witty, they swing on the boughs,
Creating a ruckus and taking their bows!

So gather around folks, for the forest's a stage,
With fables of fun that will never age.
The leaves have their laughter, the feathers their cheer,
In a world full of whimsy, there's nothing to fear!

Dance of Raindrops and Resilience

Raindrops come falling, a tap-tap delight,
Dancing on leaves in a magical sight.
"Let's twirl through the puddles!" the snails shout with glee,
While frogs leap and croak, "Just look at me!"

The ants hold a meeting on a mushroom so round,
Debating the best way to party unbound.
With tiny top hats and a crumb for the feast,
They toast under droplets, "We fancy, at least!"

Each raindrop a dancer, each splash a new thrill,
Their rhythm so catchy, the whole jungle will spill.
The toucans all join in, with a flurry of wings,
Creating a chorus that the jungle now sings!

When the skies clear up, they giggle with pride,
For they've just thrown a rain dance nobody can hide.
So next time it pours, don't you cover your head,
Join in the fun; let the raindrops be led!

Whispers Among the Canopy

In the trees, the toucans chatter,
A squirrel stole my snack, what's the matter?
The monkeys swing, they throw a shoe,
I'm not quite sure what they'll do next, too!

A parrot jokes, with colors bright,
He teases me, oh what a sight!
The frogs croak tunes, a silly band,
They croon and leap, life is just grand!

The sloths are slow, they take their time,
I tell a joke, they give a climb.
They laugh so hard, they nearly fall,
A sloth's great giggle is the best of all!

Each whisper shared among the leaves,
Is sweet laughter that never deceives.
In this jungle, so lush and bright,
We laugh a lot, from morn till night!

Echoes of Emerald Leaves

The leaves are giggling, can you hear?
A lizard slips, he shows no fear.
A chattering chipmunk wants a snack,
He sneaks up close, then darts right back!

The trees hold secrets, all a-flutter,
While ants are marching, down in the gutter.
A hedgehog dances, on tiny feet,
He tumbles down, that's quite the feat!

The river sings with splashes and splats,
While fish play games, like acrobats.
The sun peeks through, the shadows prance,
In this wild world, all creatures dance!

Each echo rings with laughter bright,
In emerald leaves, what a delight!
They share their jokes, both silly and sweet,
In this rainforest, life's a treat!

Secrets of the Amazon Canopy

Beneath the branches, secrets swirl,
A snake throws shade, gives me a twirl.
An owl hoots loudly, quite the show,
He's got his jokes, but won't let them go!

The flowers smirk, in vivid hues,
They gossip about the morning dews.
A beetle honks, it rolls a ball,
While sharing tales of the great and tall!

The bats hang out, upside-down fun,
They play charades 'til setting sun.
The pangolins roll, what a sight!
In a tangle of laughter, they take flight!

Every secret shared, in hum and buzz,
Is a cackle of fun, just because!
In the canopy high, where mischief reigns,
The Amazon whispers, in silly refrains!

Dance of the Dappled Light

In patches bright, the sunlight slips,
A monkey pirouettes, done with his flips.
He lands with a thud, and makes a face,
As the leaves shimmy, joining the race!

The caterpillars wiggle and jive,
A disco party, feels so alive!
While chattering birds sing their songs,
In this motley crew, we all belong!

The bouncy frogs leap from leaf to leaf,
Their curious jumps defy belief!
A bright butterfly spins in delight,
While dragonflies buzz in dazzling flight!

The dappled light brings joy and cheer,
As all the creatures gather near.
We spin and twirl, surround in fun,
In our wild waltz, we're never done!

Flora's Forgotten Lyrics

In a jungle bright, a flower sang,
But forgot the tune, oh what a clang!
Bees buzzed along, joining the jam,
A chorus so silly, they called it 'Ham'.

The vines swung by with a dance so neat,
Tickling toes, a comical feat.
A parrot squawked, trying to rhyme,
With laughter echoing, it was party time!

The frogs croaked loud, thinking they could rap,
With slippery moves, they fell in a flap!
While the monkeys giggled, tossing their food,
Nature's humor, oh so crude!

So there in green, amidst giggles galore,
Flora found joy, more than before.
Forgotten lyrics, but spirits so bright,
In this silly world, everything felt right!

Rhythms of Rain and Root

Raindrops tap danced on leaves so high,
While worms wiggled, under muddy sky.
They twisted and twirled, no shoes to wear,
Feeling quite fancy in wet, cool air.

Roots chuckled deep, tickling the ground,
As raindrops bounced, making a sound.
Squirrels rolled by, searching for nuts,
But slipped on slick moss, oh what big guts!

Each puddle formed a mirror of fun,
Reflections of giggles under the sun.
The jungle's beat turned wild and loud,
As creatures united, a happy crowd!

So next time rain falls, don't pout or mope,
Join in the laughter, dance without hope.
For even the storms, with boisterous cheer,
Can turn the mundane to magic, my dear!

Whispers Among the Canopy

Far above, the leaves began to chat,
A squirrel piped in, 'Who's wearing that?'
The butterflies chuckled, all in a row,
As the spiders spun tales, oh so slow.

The toucans laughed, wearing beaks of gold,
While iguanas grinned, sharing secrets untold.
"Did you hear the one about the log?"
It got up and danced, claiming it's a frog!

The trees stretched high, shaking their boughs,
As whispers of humor floated like plows.
A jungle so jolly, full of silly plots,
Who knew that green hid so many thoughts?

So take a peek, beneath the leaves,
For laughter abounds where no one believes.
In the canopy whispers, each chuckle's a gift,
In the world of the wild, spirits do lift!

Echoes in the Emerald Depths

In the depths where emerald shadows play,
A parrot joked, brightening the day.
With each cackle, the vines shook and swayed,
As creatures below hummed, 'Let's have a parade!'

The sounds of the jungle, a comedic spree,
With frogs cracking jokes, oh so carefree!
A sloth joined in, though slow and serene,
"Am I too late?" he muttered, just mean!

But the laughter erupted, like rain on the ground,
Echoes of glee, a sweet, joyful sound.
Even the shadows couldn't help but grin,
In a jungle where silliness reigns from within!

So venture into the depths of that green,
Where fun never stops, and joy is routine.
For even the echoes share in the jest,
In the heart of the woodland, we all feel blessed!

The Breath of Verdant Spirits

In the jungle, frogs wear hats,
Mocking birds sing tunes to chats.
The monkeys dance with style so fine,
While sloths just hang and sip on brine.

With vines that twist like tangled yarn,
And parakeets who gossip and warn.
A jaguar runs a joke by the trees,
While turtles giggle, "We go at ease!"

Lizards with glasses read the news,
While ants debate the best of shoes.
The caiman grins, a toothy smile,
As snakes slither past in a sassy style.

Let's toast to the fun of this grand green show,
Where every critter puts on a glow.
In this forest where laughter glides,
The breath of life is where humor resides.

Cascading Canopies at Dusk

As the sun dips, the critters sway,
Fireflies rise, joining the play.
Squirrels toss acorns far and wide,
While toucans gossip, feathers applied.

The breeze whispers through leaves so lush,
Why do sloths move in such a hush?
'Cause they're plotting, keep it on the down,
To steal the crown of the wisest clown!

If tree trunks could talk, oh what tales they'd share,
Of dance-offs between a hare and a bear.
While raccoons set up a midnight feast,
With snacks from the bins, to say the least.

So gather your laughter, join the troupe,
In this canopy where all creatures stoop.
Under the stars, let joy intertwine,
In cascading whispers, all things align.

Rain's Reverie in the Wild

Pitter-patter on leaves, what a sound,
A band of frogs jumping all around.
While puddles laugh with splashes so bright,
As turtles glide left and right.

The rain sings softly, a silly tune,
Where stripes of light start to croon.
Monkeys in hoods keep dry as they play,
While raindrops form a shower bouquet.

Beetles march like soldiers in line,
Claiming the ground as their biggest shrine.
And fish leap high in a comedy act,
For every splash, there's no need to pact!

With giggles and joy, the storm spins by,
Nature's joke as it fills the sky.
So dance through the drops, let the good times roll,
In this wild humor, we feel whole.

Harmony Amidst Foliage and Fable

In the thicket where legends dwell,
A sloth tells tales with a slow farewell.
The parrots squawk in colorful cheer,
While chattering crickets bring up the rear.

A playful spider spins webs of fun,
Dancing with flies, oh what a run!
The jaguar purrs a rhythmic beat,
While frogs in tuxedos bring the heat!

With tales of giants and tiny sprites,
The flora and fauna join for delights.
Where vines entwine in silly embrace,
And laughter blooms, in this wild space.

So frolic along with the spirits so spry,
In this foliage where humor won't die.
With every whisper of leaves and trees,
Find joy in nature's playful tease.

Melodies of the Midnight Jungle

In the night, the thief, a chatty parrot,
Sings tunes while wearing a bright green hat.
Twirling vines dance like drumsticks gone bad,
While monkeys judge the style; oh, how they spat!

Frogs play hopscotch on lily pads so fine,
While fireflies flash their disco lights in glee.
Snakes slither by, trying to join the line,
But oops! They trip; oh, what a sight to see!

A jaguar in shades reads a loud newspaper,
Claiming he's king; such drama in the trees!
But when he sneezes, all creatures start to taper,
Coughing and giggling like whispers in the breeze.

As the moon shines down, the laughter rings sweet,
In this jungle riot, silliness won't quit.
Each creature a character, making a beat,
In the forest's show, no one dares to sit!

Songs Beneath the Vines

Underneath the canopy that wobbles with cheer,
A sloth strums a coconut, thinking he's cool.
His band of ants plays maracas, oh dear!
While bees buzz along, but they think he's a fool.

A toucan yodels; there's no melody more bright,
A wild cacophony; what a peculiar night!
The bats hang upside down, juggling with delight,
While a cheeky iguana snickers at the sight.

The vines are grooving, swinging here and there,
Rhythms of laughter bubble up with the dew.
The whole jungle is moving, without any care,
And every little bumblebee joins in too!

With every giggle echoing through the trees,
The midnight party gets even more alive.
As the fun-filled chaos keeps swaying like leaves,
In this viney wonderland, all critters thrive!

The Symphony of the Wilds

In the thicket, a croc plays the sax real bold,
While turtles tap dance, shaking their shells.
A chorus of cicadas start to unfold,
Dropping the beats like tiny little bells.

A rabbit on trumpets, in suit and tie neat,
Declares it's a festival; join in the fun!
Frogs cheer him on with rhythm in their feet,
As the music swells under the rising sun.

Hummingbirds twirl like tiny ballerinas,
Fluttering around with flair and pizzazz.
An ocelot swoops in, sporting a pair of sheenas,
Skating on leaves; wow, he's quite the pizzazz!

So sway to the beat of the wild jungle flare,
Every creature's invited to join in the dance.
With giggles and tunes, no worries or care,
Just pure jungle joy, a wonderous chance!

Beneath the Rain's Embrace

Pitter patter, the rain starts to giggle,
A monkey slips by, doing the tango slide.
With puddles as mirrors, they jiggle and wiggle,
While all of the creatures find joy in the ride.

Frogs wear raincoats, colorful and bright,
Dancing on leaves, they hop without fear.
A roguish chameleon joins in the light,
Changing his colors just to tickle your ear.

The sloshing of boots on the marshy ground,
Makes every small insect clap in delight.
And cackling laughter from critters around,
Fills the air with wonders as day turns to night.

Oh, let us rejoice in this playful rain show,
As laughter and puddles go hand in hand.
Each drop a little tickle, gentle and slow,
Beneath Nature's embrace, together we stand!

The Embrace of Elements in Existence

Wet leaves giggle, they slip and slide,
The sun pops in with a goofy grin.
Raindrops dance on the grass, side to side,
While frogs croak jokes that make you spin.

Mossy rocks play their game of tag,
With ants that march in a snappy beat.
The wind whispers tales, but they all lag,
As rain threatens to dance on their feet.

Branches sway, calling squirrels for fun,
Who leap like clowns while birds steal a show.
A mischievous monkey brings out the sun,
And laughs at the puddles with a bright flow.

In this wild place where giggles ignite,
Nature's the stage and all play along.
With elements jiving in silly delight,
Existence here feels like a zany song.

Flowers Fluttering in the Fragrance

Petals flutter, like butterflies' prance,
With bees in tuxedos, they wiggle in style.
They twirl and they twine, oh what a chance,
To sip sweet nectar with a cheeky smile.

A daisy declares, 'I'm the star of the show!'
While tulips strut up with a bounce and a sway.
Lilies giggle, putting on a glow,
As pollen-packing pals come out to play.

With colors that clash like a mismatched suit,
They burst into laughter with every breeze.
Each bloom is a joker, delighting in loot,
Where fragrance and colors dance with ease.

The garden's alive with a fragrance parade,
And every flower knows how to tease.
In this floral fiesta, no need to invade,
Just join in their laughter, and chuckle with ease.

Dance of the Delicate Dews

Dew drops gather for a shimmy and shake,
A sparkling ball on the leaves that gleam.
They twirl and they spin, oh for goodness' sake,
Each drop tells a story in morning's dream.

The spider webs glisten, diamonds on show,
While crickets provide a chirpy song.
With every small splash, they all start to glow,
Nature's disco, where they all belong.

Grass blades join in with a joyful sway,
Bouncing in rhythm like a lively crew.
Even the sun joins the hilarious fray,
Casting warm glances on the dance of the dew.

So twinkle and giggle, dear friends of the morn,
For life is a dance, oh so bright and clear.
In droplets of joy, not a soul feels torn,
In this cheerful ballet, we all hold dear.

Footfalls of a Forgotten Fauna

Whispers abound in the underbrush,
A shy creature shuffles with quite the charm.
His footsteps create a delightful hush,
While shadows giggle, safe from alarm.

A wallaby hops with a comical flair,
Clumsy and giggly, he trips on a vine.
A sloth gives a salute, moves slow with care,
And laughs at the antics of those in a line.

A parrot records every silly sound,
Adding a twist with a squawk and a jeer.
Flapping around with a flair that's profound,
He mimics the snickers, spreading the cheer.

So wander, dear friends, in this wild, bright space,
Where forgotten fauna tiptoe and tease.
With jests that come out in nature's embrace,
Their footfalls remind us to laugh as we please.

Ballad of the Bejeweled Beetles

In a disco of foliage, they twist and twirl,
Beetles in sequins, giving life a whirl.
They strut with such flair, on leaves they parade,
Making the ants question their own charade.

With colors so bright, it's a vibrant show,
They dance through the branches, all laughs and no woe.
The frogs croak applause from their pads in the pond,
Wondering how such small creatures respond.

But don't let the laughter make you lose sight,
For beetles grow bold as they twinkle at night.
With each little wiggle, a giggle they bring,
In the heart of the jungle, beetles are kings.

So join in their frolic, let worries depart,
For laughter is easy when joy's in your heart.
Bejeweled and berated, they steal the main stage,
The beetles keep dancing, ageless in age!

Sounds from the Heart of the Jungle

Listen close, my friend, to the jungle's loud chat,
Where monkeys throw jokes and the parrots all bat.
The howler's a comedian, always on cue,
While bats hang around, sharing gossip anew.

There's a rustle of leaves where the capybara chill,
They gossip like teens, a popular thrill.
Crickets chirp in rhythm, a symphony sweet,
With a rhythm that keeps your heart skipping a beat.

The river says secrets as it splashes and sways,
Turtles nod wisely, imparting their ways.
The tree frogs join in with a ribbiting cheer,
Their croaks echo laughter, it's music to hear.

So venture a bit where the wild creatures dwell,
You'll find tales and giggles, a story to tell.
In the heart of the forest, the sounds dance and play,
A comedic cacophony brightens the day!

A Tapestry of Tweets in the Thicket

Up in the branches where the parrots squawk,
A tapestry woven with each little talk.
With feathers so bright and humor so grand,
They've turned the whole thicket into stand-up land.

The toucans chime in with their funny jests,
While wrens try their hand at wearing out vests.
Each tweet is a giggle, a pluck on the strings,
Bringing all of the jungle together for flings.

In a chorus of chaos, they flap and they dive,
With witty remarks, they keep laughs alive.
A ruckus of voices, a cacophony bold,
Makes the ancient trees chuckle, their stories retold.

So join in the fun, let the laughter take flight,
Be the one to share in this comic delight.
With every sweet call, the jungle's alive,
In a tapestry vibrant where joy will thrive!

Nightfall and the Nighthawk's Song

As the sun goes to bed, the night comes to play,
The nighthawk awakens, in a fanciful way.
With a wink and a nod, he begins his serenade,
A hoot and a whoop, in moonlight displayed.

With bugs buzzing high and the stars shimmering low,
He croons to the creatures, all those in the know.
The night is a riot, a hilarious bash,
With shadows all dancing, they all make a splash.

The frogs join the tune with their ribbiting tone,
While owls add their wisdom, never alone.
"Let's party!" they holler, unbothered by dawn,
Creating a ruckus till darkness is gone.

So laugh, dear friend, as night takes its reign,
For the silliness flourishes, here in the terrain.
With the nighthawk as maestro, directing the fun,
In the depths of the dark, their giggles are spun!

The Tapestry of Twilight Treads

In the forest, creatures sway,
With a squirrel prancing all the way.
Beneath the moon, the shadows play,
While turtles gossip—what a display!

Frogs wear hats while crickets sing,
A dancing bear wants to be king.
The trees all chuckle, twist, and fling,
As night unfolds its funny fling.

A sloth slides down in style so rare,
With a blink, it goes without a care.
The owls give looks, like, 'How unfair!'
While lizards chill as if a lair.

As stars peek through, their laughter stirs,
The forest hums—it never blurs.
With night as friends and bright as furs,
A wild rave where fun occurs!

Nature's Palette in Shades of Green

In a world of greens, the cheetah sneezes,
With leaves that rustle, oh, what breezes!
Parrots squawk with such expertise,
Painting laughter like skilled artists, please!

The monkeys swing with flair unmatched,
Playing tag where laughter's hatched.
With every branch, they feel dispatched,
What a scene, a comedy crafted!

A toucan tells its birdy tales,
Of zipline rides and laughing fails.
With every flap, a joke prevails,
Like raindrops slipping down the trails.

In this haven, giggles grow,
As chameleons put on quite a show.
With every hue and playful glow,
The forest's heart—oh, how they flow!

Dance of the Drizzling Dreams

When raindrops tap a jazzy beat,
The slugs all get up on their feet.
Wiggly worms join in, so sweet,
While puddles hold a funky seat.

Frogs in boots create a splash,
While butterflies have quite the clash.
A pineapple rolls with a dash,
In this downpour, no need to stash.

As clouds toss confetti, they giggle and grin,
With every raindrop, the dance begins.
Snakes wiggle on, like they've got fins,
In the rhythm of fun, no one loses spins.

So come and sway to this leafy beat,
In the rainforest, life's a treat.
With dreams that dance like a dainty feat,
Every creature finds its own heartbeat!

Stories Hidden in the Sunlight

Amidst the branches, shadowy tales,
A gecko chats as the sunlight pales.
The gossip travels down the trails,
While ants march on with tiny gales.

A butterfly learns to use a phone,
Texting the flowers, 'You'll never moan!'
While dandelions steal the throne,
In bright sunlight, hilarity's grown.

Rainbows appear with quirky flair,
As lizards blend in everywhere.
With secret whispers in the air,
The world chuckles, no room for despair.

And so the stories weave and blend,
With nature's humor, it will not end.
In every leaf, there's fun to send,
A laughter-filled bush where we all transcend!

Threads of Thought Amongst the Trees

In the canopy high, a monkey swings,
Chasing his tail as the parrot sings.
Leaves rustle softly, a playful breeze flows,
Tickling the branches, where the laughter grows.

A sloth slowly blinks, while the jaguar struts,
Wonders if he could, or if he just… nuts?
Squirrels debate what to stash for the feast,
While ants march in line, never missing a beat.

The frogs join the party, with a ribbit and croak,
Each hopping around like they're part of a joke.
The iguanas giggle as they sunbathe bright,
In this timeless hilarity, feels just right.

Here in the woods where the weirdness prevails,
Every creature's a legend, with curious tales.
So join in the fun, leave your worries behind,
In this jungle of laughter, pure joy you will find.

Timeless Echoes in the Tangle

A parrot proclaimed, 'I'm a great philosopher!'
While the sloth yawned, 'I'm the real ambassador.'
Vines twisted, laughing, as the monkeys threw fruit,
Echoes of fun danced in their playful pursuit.

Beetles stole glances, their shells glimmered bright,
While crickets composed the tunes of the night.
The rhythm was silly, but it couldn't be beat,
As the ants tapped their feet on the soft, muddy street.

A turtle soon chimed in, with a wise little grin,
'Life's just a race that we all have to win!'
Then he fell asleep, dreaming of tasty greens,
While the frogs serenaded with odd, funny scenes.

The tangle of bushes played host to the gags,
Where laughter sprouted up like blooming green rags.
A chorus of chuckles from the trees up above,
In this unforgettable dance filled with love.

Garden of Guardians and Grace

In a garden of green where the giggles bloom,
Squirrels debate if they need more room.
The flowers gossip, wearing colors so bright,
'Have you seen that snail? Is he ever in sight?'

With bugs on parade, and the butterflies dance,
In the realm of the ridiculous, they all prance.
The frogs hold a contest for the best funny face,
While the owls look confused, lost in the chase.

Lemurs swing wildly, their tails in a twirl,
As the snails throw a party, oh what a swirl!
Guardians of laughter, protecting this cheer,
With every wink shared, the joy draws near.

Each petal is precious, every bug sings along,
In this hilarious garden, where creatures belong.
A tapestry woven with humor and grace,
In this vibrant paradise, smiles fill the space.

Tides of Tranquil Treasures

On the river so serene, a fish gave a wink,
'You'll never catch me!' He took a quick pink.
As the otters dove under with giggles and splashes,
While the turtles joined in with their slow, sage dashes.

The river sang songs of laughter and cheer,
Inviting the frogs, who hopped without fear.
They floated on leaves, blowing bubbles so round,
In this joyful water, great treasure is found.

A crab did a jig, with claws held up high,
'Look at me dance, I could almost fly!'
While the dragonflies zoomed, with style and grace,
Turning the tranquil into a wild space.

Beneath the calm surface, the fun bubbles rise,
In a world full of wonders, a rare, funny prize.
So dip in the water, let troubles all cease,
For here lies the joy, in nature's sweet peace.

Melody of Mist and Moonlight

In the jungle, critters dance,
A sloth sings, gives romance.
The frogs croak in silly glee,
While toucans sip on the tea.

Bubbles pop in the stream,
Fish wear hats, it's a dream!
Monkeys play hopscotch with leaves,
Each giggle whispers and weaves.

Crickets chirp a high-pitched tune,
Bouncing hard like a buffoon.
The shadows play tag on the ground,
While owls hoot, 'Hey, get down!'

With the moon in a bright swirl,
The rainforest gives a twirl.
Party vibes in every dart,
Nature's jesters, a laugh to start!

The Treetop Chorus

Up above in the green so bright,
Birds are pitching their delight.
A parrot wears a tiny hat,
While squirrels giggle, 'Look at that!'

The wind blows tunes through the leaves,
Ticklish branches rustle, tease.
It's a concert, wild and spry,
Who needs a ticket to fly?

The drumming of ants on the trunk,
Makes the Beats sound like a funk.
While iguanas croon their dreams,
Swinging low on leafy beams.

With a laugh and a cheerful squawk,
Creatures chatter, dance, and talk.
In this jungle, we all play,
Every day's a holiday!

Lullabies of the Lush Landscape

Under the trees, a lullaby hums,
Jaguars snore, their belly drums.
A snail slips by in a soft glide,
While dreaming fish swim and slide.

As stars peek through the green canopies,
Bumblebees buzz in sweet harmonies.
The night's gentle tease brings a yawn,
Where the daylight's fun is now drawn.

Frogs in pajamas croak their sleep,
While chameleons pretend to leap.
Citronella candles flicker bright,
Even the bats giggle at night.

In the stillness, calm is the game,
Nature's lullabies, never the same.
So close your eyes, drift away,
Tomorrow brings another play!

Tangles of Twilight and Teardrops

As twilight drapes in hued delight,
Creatures gather for evening light.
Wombats wear their bow ties neat,
While dancers twirl on tiny feet.

The mist drops shades of wily glee,
A slippery slide for the bee.
Falling leaves play peek-a-boo,
While fireflies join in the view.

Silly shadows stretch and tease,
Tangled vines swing in the breeze.
The stars giggle above like sprites,
Sharing tales of wild delights.

With each churn of the night's hue,
The laughter spreads, fresh and new.
In this circus of fun, we play,
Welcoming back another day!

Serenade of the Leafy Giants

Tall trees giggle in the breeze,
Branches sway, with such great ease.
A parrot with a vibrant hat,
Sings to bugs, 'Hey, how about that?'

Vines swing low, they tease and tug,
'Catch me if you can!' they shrug.
Squirrels trade their acorn finds,
While mossy folks just stretch their minds.

A frog leaps high, a bounce and skip,
Lands in a puddle with a splashy trip.
'You got mail!' the turtle cries,
As drips fall down from cloudy skies.

The giants laugh, their leaves a-shake,
Echoing giggles for nature's sake.
With every rustle, whispers soar,
In this jungle, who could ask for more?

Shadows Danced on the Forest Floor

Shadows flicker, shimmy and sway,
As crickets plan their nightly play.
A firefly says, 'Let's light the show!'
With glowing tricks that steal the glow.

A raccoon dances, paws in the air,
His hat too big gives squirrels a scare.
They laugh and twirl around the rocks,
While owls watch, wearing puzzled socks.

Mice gather near with tiny feet,
In a line they march, oh, isn't that sweet?
Each step a giggle, each pause a cheer,
In this wild party, nothing to fear!

Stars peek down, the moon starts to grin,
As every creature shakes it in.
The forest floor, a stage so bright,
Where shadows dance till morning light!

Secrets Beneath the Verdant Veil

Underneath where no one sees,
A worm plays hide and seek with leaves.
'You can't catch me!' it winks with glee,
As ladybugs sip on herbal tea.

Roots entwine like old, sly friends,
Whispering secrets that never end.
A beetle boasts of tales untold,
While gossip spreads among the bold.

Fungi pop up with a giggle and cheer,
Sipping dew drops without any fear.
'We're the fun guys,' they tease with delight,
In this hidden world, all's merry and bright!

As night drapes close, the stories flow,
A place of laughter, where grand tales grow.
With whispers of joy just out of sight,
In the heart of green, it feels just right!

Nature's Symphony in Green

Leaves engage in a merry tune,
Strumming sounds of a croaking loon.
A symphony of chirps and flaps,
Musical insects with fancy snaps.

Hummingbirds zip with crazy speed,
Playing hopscotch, oh yes indeed!
Butterflies flutter, a dance so bright,
Their colorful wings taking flight.

The river joins with a splish and splash,
While monkeys swing, making a dash.
It's a concert where all take part,
Nature's rhythm straight from the heart.

So grab a leaf and join the crowd,
Let's make some noise, let's get loud!
In this jamboree, smiles abound,
In the embrace of green, joy is found!

www.ingramcontent.com/pod-product-compliance
Lightning Source LLC
Chambersburg PA
CBHW051645160426
43209CB00004B/795